45 Strawberry Recipes for Home

By: Kelly Johnson

Table of Contents

- Strawberry Shortcake
- Fresh Strawberry Pie
- Strawberry Cheesecake
- Homemade Strawberry Jam
- Strawberry Smoothie Bowl
- Strawberry Banana Bread
- Chocolate Covered Strawberries
- Strawberry Greek Yogurt Popsicles
- Strawberry Spinach Salad with Balsamic Vinaigrette
- Strawberry Basil Lemonade
- Strawberry Mango Salsa
- Strawberry Avocado Toast
- Strawberry and Goat Cheese Bruschetta
- Strawberry Almond Overnight Oats
- Strawberry Balsamic Glazed Chicken
- Grilled Strawberry Caprese Salad
- Strawberry Cobbler
- Strawberry Sorbet
- Strawberry Balsamic Flatbread
- Strawberry and Cream Stuffed French Toast
- Strawberry Chia Seed Pudding
- Strawberry Brie Quesadillas
- Strawberry and Feta Salad with Mint
- Strawberry Margarita
- Strawberry and Cucumber Gazpacho
- Strawberry Ricotta Pancakes
- Strawberry Balsamic Grilled Cheese
- Strawberry Basil Chicken
- Strawberry Lemon Muffins
- Strawberry Pistachio Energy Bites
- Strawberry and Spinach Stuffed Chicken Breast
- Strawberry Coconut Chia Popsicles
- Strawberry and Goat Cheese Grilled Pizza
- Strawberry Balsamic Glazed Salmon
- Strawberry and Cream Cheese Stuffed French Toast Casserole

- Strawberry Rhubarb Crisp
- Strawberry and Avocado Chicken Salad
- Strawberry and Pecan Quinoa Salad
- Strawberry and Nutella Crepes
- Strawberry Basil Lemon Sorbet
- Strawberry Cinnamon Rolls
- Strawberry and Almond Butter Smoothie
- Strawberry Pistachio Salad
- Strawberry and Balsamic Bruschetta
- Strawberry Tiramisu

Strawberry Shortcake

Ingredients:

- 1 pound fresh strawberries, hulled and sliced
- 1/4 cup granulated sugar
- 2 cups all-purpose flour
- 1/4 cup granulated sugar
- 1 tablespoon baking powder
- 1/2 teaspoon salt
- 1/2 cup unsalted butter, cold and cut into small pieces
- 2/3 cup whole milk
- 1 teaspoon vanilla extract
- 1 cup heavy cream
- 2 tablespoons powdered sugar
- Fresh mint leaves for garnish (optional)

Instructions:

Prepare the Strawberries:
- In a bowl, combine the sliced strawberries and 1/4 cup of granulated sugar. Toss to coat the strawberries evenly, then set aside to macerate for at least 30 minutes.

Make the Shortcakes:
- Preheat the oven to 425°F (220°C).
- In a large mixing bowl, whisk together the flour, 1/4 cup of granulated sugar, baking powder, and salt.
- Add the cold, cubed butter to the flour mixture. Using a pastry cutter or your fingers, cut the butter into the flour until the mixture resembles coarse crumbs.
- Pour in the milk and vanilla extract, stirring until just combined. Do not overmix.
- Turn the dough out onto a floured surface and pat it into a 1-inch thick rectangle. Use a round biscuit cutter to cut out shortcakes and place them on a baking sheet lined with parchment paper.
- Bake for 12-15 minutes or until golden brown. Allow the shortcakes to cool slightly.

Whip the Cream:

- In a separate bowl, whip the heavy cream and powdered sugar until stiff peaks form.

Assemble the Strawberry Shortcakes:
- Slice the cooled shortcakes in half horizontally.
- Spoon a generous portion of macerated strawberries onto the bottom half of each shortcake.
- Dollop a spoonful of whipped cream over the strawberries.
- Place the other half of the shortcake on top, creating a sandwich.
- Garnish with additional whipped cream and a sprig of fresh mint if desired.

Serve:
- Serve immediately and enjoy the delightful combination of sweet, juicy strawberries, tender shortcake, and billowy whipped cream.

This classic Strawberry Shortcake recipe is a perfect way to showcase the bright and fresh flavors of ripe strawberries. It's a timeless dessert that's simple to make and sure to be a crowd-pleaser.

Fresh Strawberry Pie

Ingredients:

For the Crust:

- 1 1/2 cups graham cracker crumbs
- 1/3 cup melted butter
- 1/4 cup sugar

For the Filling:

- 4 cups fresh strawberries, hulled and halved
- 1 cup sugar
- 3 tablespoons cornstarch
- 1/4 teaspoon salt
- 1/2 cup water
- 1 teaspoon lemon juice
- 1 teaspoon vanilla extract

For the Whipped Cream:

- 1 cup heavy cream
- 2 tablespoons powdered sugar
- 1 teaspoon vanilla extract

Instructions:

1. Preparing the Crust:

- In a bowl, combine graham cracker crumbs, melted butter, and sugar.
- Press the mixture into a 9-inch pie dish to form the crust.
- Chill the crust in the refrigerator while preparing the filling.

2. Making the Filling:

- In a saucepan, mash 1 cup of strawberries. Add sugar, cornstarch, and salt. Mix well.
- Gradually stir in water and bring the mixture to a boil over medium heat, stirring constantly.

- Cook until the mixture thickens. Remove from heat and let it cool slightly.
- Stir in lemon juice and vanilla extract.
- Gently fold in the remaining fresh strawberries.
- Pour the strawberry filling into the prepared crust.

3. Chilling the Pie:

- Refrigerate the pie for at least 4 hours or until set.

4. Making the Whipped Cream:

- In a chilled bowl, whip the heavy cream until it starts to thicken.
- Add powdered sugar and vanilla extract, then continue whipping until stiff peaks form.

5. Serving:

- Once the pie is set, top it with a generous layer of whipped cream before serving.

Enjoy your delicious Fresh Strawberry Pie!

Strawberry Cheesecake

Ingredients:

For the Crust:

- 1 1/2 cups graham cracker crumbs
- 1/4 cup sugar
- 1/2 cup melted butter

For the Cheesecake Filling:

- 4 packages (32 ounces) cream cheese, softened
- 1 1/4 cups sugar
- 1 teaspoon vanilla extract
- 4 large eggs
- 2/3 cup sour cream
- 2/3 cup heavy cream

For the Strawberry Topping:

- 2 cups fresh strawberries, hulled and sliced
- 1/4 cup sugar
- 1 teaspoon lemon juice

Instructions:

1. Preparing the Crust:

- In a bowl, combine graham cracker crumbs, sugar, and melted butter.
- Press the mixture into the bottom of a 9-inch springform pan to form the crust.
- Chill the crust in the refrigerator while preparing the filling.

2. Making the Cheesecake Filling:

- Preheat the oven to 325°F (163°C).
- In a large mixing bowl, beat the cream cheese until smooth.
- Add sugar and vanilla extract, and beat until well combined.
- Add eggs one at a time, beating well after each addition.
- Fold in sour cream and heavy cream until the batter is smooth.

- Pour the cheesecake batter over the prepared crust.

3. Baking the Cheesecake:

    - Bake in the preheated oven for about 55-65 minutes or until the center is set and the top is lightly browned.
    - Allow the cheesecake to cool in the oven with the door ajar for about 1 hour.
    - Refrigerate the cheesecake for at least 4 hours or overnight.

4. Making the Strawberry Topping:

    - In a saucepan, combine sliced strawberries, sugar, and lemon juice.
    - Cook over medium heat until the strawberries release their juices and the mixture thickens slightly.
    - Let the strawberry topping cool.

5. Assembling and Serving:

    - Once the cheesecake is chilled, spread the strawberry topping over the top.
    - Remove the cheesecake from the springform pan and transfer it to a serving plate.

Enjoy your delicious Strawberry Cheesecake!

Homemade Strawberry Jam

Ingredients:

- 4 cups fresh strawberries, hulled and chopped
- 3 cups granulated sugar
- 1/4 cup lemon juice
- 1 packet (about 1.75 oz) fruit pectin

Instructions:

1. Prepare the Strawberries:

- Wash the strawberries thoroughly and remove the stems. Chop the strawberries into small pieces.

2. Sterilize Jars:

- Wash glass jars and lids in hot, soapy water. Sterilize them by placing the jars in a boiling water bath for 10 minutes. Allow them to air dry.

3. Cook the Strawberries:

- In a large, non-reactive saucepan, combine the chopped strawberries, sugar, and lemon juice. Stir well to combine.
- Let the mixture sit for about 15 minutes to allow the sugar to dissolve and the strawberries to release their juices.

4. Cook the Jam:

- After the strawberries have macerated, place the saucepan over medium-high heat. Bring the mixture to a boil, stirring frequently.
- Once boiling, add the fruit pectin and continue to stir. Boil for 10-15 minutes or until the jam reaches the desired consistency. You can test the consistency by placing a small amount on a cold plate – it should gel as it cools.

5. Skim Foam (Optional):

- If there's any foam on the surface of the jam, skim it off with a spoon.

6. Jar and Seal:

    - Ladle the hot jam into the sterilized jars, leaving about 1/4-inch headspace. Wipe the rims of the jars with a clean, damp cloth.
    - Place the sterilized lids on the jars and screw on the metal bands until they are fingertip-tight.

7. Water Bath Canning (Optional):

    - Process the jars in a boiling water bath for 10 minutes to ensure they are sealed properly. Make sure the water covers the jars by at least an inch.

8. Cool and Store:

    - Allow the jars to cool completely on a clean kitchen towel or cooling rack.
    - Once cooled, check that the lids have sealed properly by pressing down on the center of each lid. If it doesn't pop back, the jar is sealed. If it does pop back, store that jar in the refrigerator.

9. Enjoy:

    - Store the sealed jars in a cool, dark place. Once opened, keep the jam in the refrigerator.

Now you have delicious Homemade Strawberry Jam to enjoy on toast, with yogurt, or in your favorite recipes!

Strawberry Smoothie Bowl

Ingredients:

For the Smoothie:

- 1 1/2 cups frozen strawberries
- 1 ripe banana, frozen
- 1/2 cup plain Greek yogurt
- 1/2 cup almond milk (or any milk of your choice)
- 1 tablespoon honey or maple syrup (optional for sweetness)
- 1/2 teaspoon vanilla extract (optional)

Toppings:

- Sliced fresh strawberries
- Granola
- Chia seeds
- Shredded coconut
- Sliced banana
- Honey or maple syrup for drizzling

Instructions:

1. Prepare the Smoothie:

- In a blender, combine the frozen strawberries, frozen banana, Greek yogurt, almond milk, honey (if using), and vanilla extract.
- Blend until smooth and creamy. If the mixture is too thick, you can add more almond milk in small increments until you reach your desired consistency.

2. Assemble the Bowl:

- Pour the smoothie into a bowl.

3. Add Toppings:

- Arrange the sliced fresh strawberries, granola, chia seeds, shredded coconut, and sliced banana on top of the smoothie.

4. Drizzle with Sweetener (Optional):

- Drizzle honey or maple syrup over the toppings for added sweetness.

5. Enjoy:

- Grab a spoon and enjoy your delicious and nutritious Strawberry Smoothie Bowl!

Feel free to customize the toppings based on your preferences. This smoothie bowl is not only visually appealing but also a delightful way to start your day or enjoy a healthy snack.

Strawberry Banana Bread

Ingredients:

- 1 3/4 cups all-purpose flour
- 1 teaspoon baking powder
- 1/2 teaspoon baking soda
- 1/2 teaspoon salt
- 1/2 cup unsalted butter, softened
- 1 cup granulated sugar
- 2 large eggs
- 1 teaspoon vanilla extract
- 3 ripe bananas, mashed
- 1 cup fresh strawberries, diced
- 1/2 cup plain Greek yogurt (or sour cream)
- 1/2 cup chopped nuts (walnuts or pecans), optional

Instructions:

Preheat the Oven:
- Preheat your oven to 350°F (175°C). Grease and flour a 9x5-inch loaf pan.

Dry Ingredients:
- In a medium bowl, whisk together the flour, baking powder, baking soda, and salt. Set aside.

Cream Butter and Sugar:
- In a large mixing bowl, cream together the softened butter and granulated sugar until light and fluffy.

Add Eggs and Vanilla:
- Add the eggs one at a time, beating well after each addition. Stir in the vanilla extract.

Mash Bananas:
- Mash the ripe bananas with a fork and add them to the wet ingredients. Mix until well combined.

Alternate Dry Ingredients and Yogurt:
- Gradually add the dry ingredients to the banana mixture, alternating with the Greek yogurt. Begin and end with the dry ingredients. Mix until just combined.

Fold in Strawberries and Nuts:

- Gently fold in the diced strawberries and chopped nuts (if using).

Bake:
- Pour the batter into the prepared loaf pan and spread it evenly. Bake in the preheated oven for 60-70 minutes or until a toothpick inserted into the center comes out clean.

Cool:
- Allow the banana bread to cool in the pan for about 10 minutes, then transfer it to a wire rack to cool completely.

Slice and Serve:
- Once cooled, slice the Strawberry Banana Bread and serve. Enjoy!

This Strawberry Banana Bread is a delightful twist on the classic banana bread, adding the sweetness and freshness of strawberries. Feel free to customize it by adding your favorite nuts or even a drizzle of glaze if desired.

Chocolate Covered Strawberries

Ingredients:

- 1 pound fresh strawberries, washed and dried
- 8 ounces semisweet or bittersweet chocolate, chopped (or use chocolate chips)
- 1 tablespoon coconut oil or vegetable shortening (optional, for smoother consistency)
- Toppings (optional): chopped nuts, shredded coconut, sprinkles, etc.

Instructions:

Prepare Strawberries:
- Make sure the strawberries are completely dry. Line a baking sheet with parchment paper or wax paper.

Melt Chocolate:
- In a heatproof bowl, melt the chocolate in the microwave in 30-second intervals, stirring well after each interval. Alternatively, you can melt the chocolate using a double boiler on the stovetop.

Add Coconut Oil (Optional):
- If you want a smoother consistency for the chocolate, you can add coconut oil or vegetable shortening to the melted chocolate and stir until well combined.

Dip Strawberries:
- Hold a strawberry by the stem and dip it into the melted chocolate, swirling to coat it evenly. Allow excess chocolate to drip off.

Add Toppings (Optional):
- If you're adding toppings like chopped nuts or shredded coconut, sprinkle them over the chocolate-covered strawberry while the chocolate is still wet.

Place on Baking Sheet:
- Place the dipped strawberries on the prepared baking sheet, making sure they are not touching each other.

Cool and Set:
- Allow the chocolate-covered strawberries to cool and set at room temperature. You can speed up the process by placing them in the refrigerator for about 15-20 minutes.

Serve:

- Once the chocolate is set, transfer the strawberries to a serving plate and enjoy!

Chocolate Covered Strawberries make for a delightful treat and are perfect for special occasions or as a sweet snack. Get creative with different toppings or drizzle additional melted chocolate for extra indulgence!

Strawberry Greek Yogurt Popsicles

Ingredients:

- 1 cup fresh strawberries, hulled and halved
- 1 tablespoon honey or maple syrup (adjust to taste)
- 1 cup Greek yogurt (plain or vanilla)
- 1/2 teaspoon vanilla extract (if using plain yogurt)
- Popsicle molds

Instructions:

Prepare Strawberries:
- In a blender or food processor, puree the fresh strawberries until smooth. If you prefer some texture, you can leave it slightly chunky.

Sweeten the Strawberry Puree:
- Taste the strawberry puree and sweeten it with honey or maple syrup according to your preference. Blend again to combine.

Prepare Yogurt Mixture:
- In a separate bowl, mix the Greek yogurt with vanilla extract if you're using plain yogurt. If you're using vanilla-flavored Greek yogurt, you can skip the extract.

Layering:
- Spoon a layer of strawberry puree into each popsicle mold, filling them about one-third of the way.
- Add a layer of Greek yogurt on top of the strawberry puree, filling another third of the mold.
- Continue alternating layers until the molds are almost full, finishing with a layer of strawberry puree.

Swirl:
- Use a popsicle stick or a skewer to gently swirl the layers for a marbled effect.

Insert Sticks:
- Insert popsicle sticks into the molds, ensuring they are centered.

Freeze:
- Place the popsicle molds in the freezer and let them freeze for at least 4-6 hours or until completely solid.

Unmold and Enjoy:

- Once frozen, run the molds under warm water for a few seconds to release the popsicles. Enjoy your homemade Strawberry Greek Yogurt Popsicles!

These popsicles are a delicious and healthy treat, perfect for hot days or as a guilt-free dessert. Feel free to customize by adding other fruits or experimenting with different yogurt flavors.

Strawberry Spinach Salad with Balsamic Vinaigrette

Ingredients:

For the Salad:

- 6 cups fresh baby spinach, washed and dried
- 1 pint fresh strawberries, hulled and sliced
- 1/2 cup feta cheese, crumbled
- 1/4 cup red onion, thinly sliced
- 1/4 cup slivered almonds, toasted

For the Balsamic Vinaigrette:

- 1/4 cup balsamic vinegar
- 1/3 cup extra-virgin olive oil
- 1 tablespoon Dijon mustard
- 1 tablespoon honey
- Salt and black pepper, to taste

Instructions:

1. Prepare the Salad:

- In a large salad bowl, combine the baby spinach, sliced strawberries, crumbled feta cheese, sliced red onion, and toasted slivered almonds.

2. Make the Balsamic Vinaigrette:

- In a small bowl, whisk together balsamic vinegar, olive oil, Dijon mustard, honey, salt, and black pepper until well combined.

3. Dress the Salad:

- Drizzle the balsamic vinaigrette over the salad.

4. Toss Gently:

- Toss the salad gently to ensure the dressing coats all the ingredients evenly.

5. Serve:

- Divide the salad among plates or serve it in a large bowl.

6. Garnish:

- Optionally, you can garnish with additional feta cheese and almonds.

7. Enjoy:

- Serve immediately and enjoy this fresh and flavorful Strawberry Spinach Salad!

This salad is a perfect blend of sweet strawberries, savory feta, and crunchy almonds, all brought together by a tangy balsamic vinaigrette. It makes for a light and delicious side dish or a refreshing lunch option.

Strawberry Basil Lemonade

Ingredients:

- 1 cup fresh strawberries, hulled and halved
- 1/2 cup fresh basil leaves
- 1 cup freshly squeezed lemon juice (about 4-6 lemons)
- 1/2 cup granulated sugar (adjust to taste)
- 4 cups cold water
- Ice cubes
- Lemon slices and fresh basil leaves for garnish

Instructions:

1. Prepare the Strawberry Basil Infusion:

- In a blender, combine fresh strawberries and basil leaves. Blend until smooth.

2. Make the Lemonade Base:

- In a pitcher, combine the freshly squeezed lemon juice and granulated sugar. Stir well until the sugar is dissolved.

3. Combine Ingredients:

- Pour the strawberry basil puree into the pitcher with the lemonade base. Stir to combine.

4. Add Cold Water:

- Pour in the cold water and stir again. Taste and adjust the sweetness if needed by adding more sugar.

5. Chill:

- Refrigerate the lemonade for at least 1-2 hours to allow the flavors to meld.

6. Strain (Optional):

- If you prefer a smoother consistency, you can strain the lemonade to remove the strawberry and basil pulp. Use a fine mesh strainer or cheesecloth.

7. Serve:

- Fill glasses with ice cubes and pour the Strawberry Basil Lemonade over the ice.

8. Garnish:

- Garnish each glass with a slice of lemon and a fresh basil leaf.

9. Enjoy:

- Refresh yourself with this delightful Strawberry Basil Lemonade!

This homemade lemonade combines the sweet and vibrant flavors of strawberries with the herbal freshness of basil, creating a deliciously unique and refreshing drink. Perfect for warm days or as a delightful addition to any gathering!

Strawberry Mango Salsa

Ingredients:

- 1 cup diced strawberries
- 1 cup diced mango
- 1/2 cup diced red onion
- 1/2 cup chopped fresh cilantro
- 1 jalapeño, seeds removed and finely chopped (adjust to taste)
- 1 lime, juiced
- Salt and pepper to taste

Instructions:

Prepare the Ingredients:
- Wash and hull the strawberries. Dice the strawberries and mango into small, uniform pieces.
- Finely chop the red onion, jalapeño, and fresh cilantro.

Combine Ingredients:
- In a bowl, combine the diced strawberries, diced mango, chopped red onion, jalapeño, and fresh cilantro.

Add Lime Juice:
- Squeeze the juice of one lime over the mixture. Adjust the amount of lime juice to taste.

Season:
- Season the salsa with salt and pepper. Stir gently to combine all the ingredients.

Chill (Optional):
- For enhanced flavor, refrigerate the salsa for about 30 minutes to allow the flavors to meld. This step is optional, and you can serve it immediately if desired.

Serve:
- Serve the Strawberry Mango Salsa with tortilla chips, as a topping for grilled chicken or fish, or as a refreshing side dish.

Enjoy:
- Enjoy the vibrant and fruity flavors of this Strawberry Mango Salsa!

This salsa is a perfect balance of sweet and tangy, making it a delightful accompaniment to various dishes or a tasty snack on its own.

Strawberry Avocado Toast

Ingredients:

- 2 slices of whole-grain bread
- 1 ripe avocado
- 1 cup fresh strawberries, hulled and sliced
- 1 tablespoon balsamic glaze
- 1 tablespoon extra-virgin olive oil
- Salt and pepper to taste
- Optional toppings: feta cheese, microgreens, or a drizzle of honey

Instructions:

Toast the Bread:
- Toast the slices of whole-grain bread to your desired level of crispiness.

Prepare Avocado Spread:
- While the bread is toasting, mash the ripe avocado in a bowl. Add a pinch of salt and pepper and mix well.

Spread Avocado on Toast:
- Once the bread is toasted, spread the mashed avocado evenly over each slice.

Add Sliced Strawberries:
- Arrange the sliced strawberries on top of the mashed avocado.

Drizzle Balsamic Glaze and Olive Oil:
- Drizzle balsamic glaze and extra-virgin olive oil over the strawberries and avocado.

Season and Add Optional Toppings:
- Sprinkle a bit of salt and pepper over the top. If desired, add optional toppings such as crumbled feta cheese, microgreens, or a drizzle of honey for added flavor.

Serve and Enjoy:
- Serve the Strawberry Avocado Toast immediately while the bread is still warm. Enjoy this delightful and nutritious breakfast or snack!

This Strawberry Avocado Toast offers a perfect combination of creamy avocado, sweet strawberries, and a hint of balsamic glaze, creating a delicious and satisfying treat. Feel free to customize it with your favorite toppings and enjoy a burst of flavors with every bite.

Strawberry and Goat Cheese Bruschetta

Ingredients:

- Baguette, thinly sliced
- 1 cup fresh strawberries, hulled and diced
- 4 ounces goat cheese
- 2 tablespoons balsamic glaze
- Fresh basil leaves, thinly sliced
- Honey for drizzling (optional)
- Olive oil for brushing the bread
- Salt and pepper to taste

Instructions:

Preheat the Oven:
- Preheat your oven to 375°F (190°C).

Prepare Baguette Slices:
- Arrange the thinly sliced baguette on a baking sheet. Brush each slice with olive oil.

Toast the Baguette:
- Toast the baguette slices in the preheated oven for about 5-7 minutes or until they are golden and crisp. Remove from the oven and let them cool slightly.

Prepare Strawberry and Goat Cheese Mixture:
- In a bowl, gently mix the diced strawberries with crumbled goat cheese. Add a pinch of salt and pepper to taste.

Assemble Bruschetta:
- Spoon the strawberry and goat cheese mixture onto each toasted baguette slice.

Drizzle Balsamic Glaze:
- Drizzle balsamic glaze over each bruschetta.

Garnish with Basil and Honey (Optional):
- Sprinkle thinly sliced fresh basil leaves over the top. If desired, drizzle a bit of honey for sweetness.

Serve Immediately:
- Serve the Strawberry and Goat Cheese Bruschetta immediately, allowing the flavors to shine while the bread is still warm.

This Strawberry and Goat Cheese Bruschetta is a perfect blend of sweet and savory, with the creaminess of goat cheese complementing the freshness of strawberries. It makes for an elegant appetizer or a delightful snack for any occasion. Enjoy!

Strawberry Almond Overnight Oats

Ingredients:

- 1/2 cup rolled oats
- 1/2 cup almond milk (or any milk of your choice)
- 1/2 cup fresh strawberries, sliced
- 1 tablespoon chia seeds
- 1 tablespoon almond butter
- 1 teaspoon honey (optional, for sweetness)
- 1/4 teaspoon almond extract (optional)
- Sliced almonds for topping

Instructions:

Combine Ingredients:
- In a mason jar or airtight container, combine rolled oats, almond milk, sliced strawberries, chia seeds, almond butter, honey (if using), and almond extract (if using).

Mix Well:
- Stir the ingredients well until everything is evenly combined.

Refrigerate Overnight:
- Seal the container and refrigerate it overnight, or for at least 4-6 hours. This allows the oats and chia seeds to absorb the liquid and soften.

Top with Almonds:
- Before serving, give the mixture a good stir. Top the oats with sliced almonds for added crunch.

Optional Garnish:
- If desired, you can add a few extra sliced strawberries or a drizzle of almond butter on top before serving.

Enjoy:
- Enjoy your Strawberry Almond Overnight Oats straight from the jar or transfer them to a bowl. These oats can be eaten cold or warmed up in the microwave, depending on your preference.

This Strawberry Almond Overnight Oats recipe is not only delicious but also a convenient and nutritious breakfast option. It's packed with fiber, protein, and the natural sweetness of strawberries. Feel free to customize it with your favorite toppings or additional fruits.

Strawberry Balsamic Glazed Chicken

Ingredients:

- 4 boneless, skinless chicken breasts
- Salt and black pepper, to taste
- 1 tablespoon olive oil
- 1/2 cup balsamic vinegar
- 1/4 cup strawberry jam or preserves
- 1 tablespoon Dijon mustard
- 1 teaspoon soy sauce
- 1 teaspoon minced garlic
- 1/2 teaspoon dried thyme (optional)
- Fresh strawberries for garnish
- Fresh basil leaves for garnish

Instructions:

Season Chicken:
- Season the chicken breasts with salt and black pepper on both sides.

Sear Chicken:
- Heat olive oil in a large skillet over medium-high heat. Sear the chicken breasts for about 4-5 minutes on each side or until golden brown and cooked through. Remove the chicken from the skillet and set aside.

Prepare Glaze:
- In the same skillet, add balsamic vinegar, strawberry jam, Dijon mustard, soy sauce, minced garlic, and dried thyme (if using). Whisk the ingredients together over medium heat until the sauce thickens slightly, about 3-4 minutes.

Glaze Chicken:
- Return the seared chicken breasts to the skillet, coating them with the strawberry balsamic glaze. Cook for an additional 2-3 minutes, allowing the chicken to absorb the flavors of the glaze.

Check for Doneness:
- Ensure the chicken is cooked through (reaches an internal temperature of 165°F or 74°C).

Serve:

- Transfer the glazed chicken to a serving platter. Spoon any extra glaze over the top.

Garnish:
- Garnish with fresh strawberries and basil leaves for a burst of freshness and color.

Enjoy:
- Serve the Strawberry Balsamic Glazed Chicken with your favorite side dishes, such as rice, quinoa, or roasted vegetables.

This dish combines the sweetness of strawberries with the tanginess of balsamic vinegar, creating a flavorful glaze for succulent chicken breasts. It's a delightful and elegant recipe that's perfect for a special dinner or a weekend treat.

Grilled Strawberry Caprese Salad

Ingredients:

- 1 pint fresh strawberries, hulled and halved
- 1 cup cherry tomatoes, halved
- 8 ounces fresh mozzarella, sliced
- Balsamic glaze (store-bought or homemade)
- Fresh basil leaves, torn
- Extra-virgin olive oil
- Salt and black pepper, to taste

Instructions:

Preheat the Grill:
- Preheat your grill to medium-high heat.

Prepare Ingredients:
- Hull and halve the fresh strawberries.
- Halve the cherry tomatoes.
- Slice the fresh mozzarella.

Grill Strawberries:
- Lightly brush the strawberry halves with olive oil.
- Place the strawberries on the preheated grill and cook for about 2-3 minutes on each side until grill marks appear. Remove from the grill and set aside.

Assemble Salad:
- On a serving platter, arrange the grilled strawberries, cherry tomatoes, and fresh mozzarella slices.

Drizzle with Balsamic Glaze:
- Drizzle balsamic glaze over the salad. You can use store-bought balsamic glaze or make your own by reducing balsamic vinegar with a bit of honey until it thickens.

Season and Garnish:
- Sprinkle salt and black pepper over the salad to taste.
- Tear fresh basil leaves and scatter them over the top.

Finish with Olive Oil:
- Drizzle extra-virgin olive oil over the salad for added richness.

Serve:

- Serve the Grilled Strawberry Caprese Salad immediately as a refreshing and flavorful side dish.

This Grilled Strawberry Caprese Salad is a delightful twist on the classic Caprese, adding a hint of smokiness from the grilled strawberries. It's a perfect dish to enjoy during the warmer months when strawberries are in season.

Strawberry Sorbet

Ingredients:

- 4 cups fresh strawberries, hulled
- 1 cup granulated sugar
- 1/4 cup fresh lemon juice (about 2 lemons)
- 1 cup water

Instructions:

Prepare Strawberries:
- Wash and hull the fresh strawberries.

Make Simple Syrup:
- In a saucepan, combine sugar and water. Heat over medium heat, stirring until the sugar completely dissolves. Allow it to cool.

Blend Strawberries:
- In a blender or food processor, blend the hulled strawberries until smooth.

Combine Strawberry Puree and Simple Syrup:
- In a mixing bowl, combine the strawberry puree with the cooled simple syrup. Stir well to ensure even mixing.

Add Lemon Juice:
- Squeeze fresh lemon juice and add it to the strawberry mixture. Stir to combine.

Chill the Mixture:
- Refrigerate the strawberry mixture for at least 2 hours or until it's thoroughly chilled.

Freeze:
- Pour the chilled strawberry mixture into an ice cream maker and churn according to the manufacturer's instructions until it reaches a sorbet consistency.

Serve or Freeze:
- You can serve the strawberry sorbet immediately for a soft-serve texture, or transfer it to a lidded container and freeze for a few hours for a firmer texture.

Enjoy:
- Scoop the Strawberry Sorbet into bowls or cones and enjoy this refreshing and fruity frozen treat!

This Strawberry Sorbet is a perfect way to enjoy the natural sweetness of fresh strawberries in a cool and satisfying dessert. It's easy to make and doesn't require any special equipment other than an ice cream maker.

Strawberry Balsamic Flatbread

Ingredients:

For the Flatbread:

- 1 pound pizza dough (store-bought or homemade)
- Olive oil for brushing

For the Toppings:

- 1 cup fresh strawberries, hulled and sliced
- 1/2 cup balsamic glaze (store-bought or homemade)
- 1 cup mozzarella cheese, shredded
- 1/4 cup goat cheese, crumbled
- Fresh basil leaves for garnish
- Balsamic reduction for drizzling (optional)

Instructions:

Preheat the Oven:
- Preheat your oven according to the pizza dough instructions or around 450°F (230°C).

Prepare the Flatbread:
- Roll out the pizza dough on a floured surface to your desired thickness.

Brush with Olive Oil:
- Place the rolled-out dough on a baking sheet or pizza stone. Brush the surface with olive oil to prevent it from getting soggy.

Add Toppings:
- Sprinkle the shredded mozzarella evenly over the dough. Distribute the sliced strawberries and crumbled goat cheese on top.

Bake:
- Bake in the preheated oven according to the pizza dough instructions or until the crust is golden brown and the cheese is melted and bubbly.

Drizzle Balsamic Glaze:
- Once out of the oven, drizzle the balsamic glaze over the flatbread.

Garnish:
- Garnish with fresh basil leaves for a burst of flavor and aroma.

Optional Drizzle:

- If desired, you can add an extra drizzle of balsamic reduction for added richness.

Slice and Serve:
  - Allow the flatbread to cool for a few minutes, then slice it into portions and serve.

This Strawberry Balsamic Flatbread combines the sweetness of fresh strawberries with the savory notes of balsamic glaze and the creaminess of goat cheese. It's a delightful and unique twist on traditional flatbread and makes for a perfect appetizer or light meal.

Strawberry and Cream Stuffed French Toast

Ingredients:

For the Stuffed French Toast:

- 8 slices of thick-cut bread (such as brioche or challah)
- 1 cup cream cheese, softened
- 1/4 cup powdered sugar
- 1 teaspoon vanilla extract
- 1 cup fresh strawberries, hulled and sliced
- 4 large eggs
- 1 cup milk
- 1 teaspoon ground cinnamon
- Butter for cooking

For Topping:

- Fresh strawberries, sliced
- Maple syrup
- Powdered sugar (optional)

Instructions:

Prepare the Cream Cheese Filling:
- In a bowl, mix the softened cream cheese, powdered sugar, and vanilla extract until smooth.

Assemble the Sandwiches:
- Spread a generous amount of the cream cheese mixture onto one side of each bread slice. Place a layer of sliced strawberries on half of the slices. Top with the remaining slices to create sandwiches.

Prepare the Egg Mixture:
- In a shallow bowl, whisk together the eggs, milk, and ground cinnamon.

Dip and Coat:
- Carefully dip each sandwich into the egg mixture, ensuring both sides are coated.

Cook the French Toast:

- In a skillet or griddle, melt butter over medium heat. Cook the stuffed French toast sandwiches until golden brown on both sides and the filling is warm and slightly melty.

Serve:
- Place the stuffed French toast on a serving plate. Top with additional sliced strawberries, a drizzle of maple syrup, and a dusting of powdered sugar if desired.

Enjoy:
- Serve the Strawberry and Cream Stuffed French Toast while warm. Enjoy the delicious combination of creamy filling, sweet strawberries, and perfectly cooked French toast.

This Strawberry and Cream Stuffed French Toast is a delightful breakfast or brunch option, combining the richness of cream cheese with the sweetness of fresh strawberries. It's sure to be a hit at your table!

Strawberry Chia Seed Pudding

Ingredients:

- 1 cup fresh strawberries, hulled and sliced
- 2 tablespoons maple syrup or honey
- 1 teaspoon vanilla extract
- 1/3 cup chia seeds
- 1 1/2 cups almond milk (or any milk of your choice)
- Optional toppings: sliced strawberries, chopped nuts, or shredded coconut

Instructions:

Prepare the Strawberry Puree:
- In a blender or food processor, blend the fresh strawberries, maple syrup (or honey), and vanilla extract until smooth.

Combine Chia Seeds and Strawberry Puree:
- In a bowl, mix the chia seeds with the strawberry puree. Stir well to ensure the chia seeds are evenly coated.

Add Almond Milk:
- Pour in the almond milk and continue stirring the mixture to prevent clumps of chia seeds from forming.

Refrigerate Overnight:
- Cover the bowl and refrigerate the mixture for at least 4 hours or, preferably, overnight. This allows the chia seeds to absorb the liquid and create a pudding-like consistency.

Stir Before Serving:
- Before serving, give the pudding a good stir to make sure the chia seeds are evenly distributed.

Serve with Toppings:
- Divide the strawberry chia seed pudding into serving glasses or bowls. Top with additional sliced strawberries, chopped nuts, or shredded coconut if desired.

Enjoy:
- Enjoy this nutritious and flavorful Strawberry Chia Seed Pudding as a healthy breakfast, snack, or dessert.

This pudding is not only delicious but also packed with the nutritional benefits of chia seeds and fresh strawberries. It's a delightful and satisfying treat!

Strawberry Brie Quesadillas

Ingredients:

- 4 large flour tortillas
- 8 ounces Brie cheese, rind removed and sliced
- 1 cup fresh strawberries, hulled and sliced
- 2 tablespoons balsamic glaze
- 2 tablespoons honey
- Fresh basil leaves for garnish (optional)
- Olive oil for brushing

Instructions:

Prepare Ingredients:
- Hull and slice the fresh strawberries.
- Remove the rind from the Brie cheese and slice it into thin pieces.

Assemble Quesadillas:
- Place a tortilla on a flat surface. Arrange slices of Brie cheese evenly over half of the tortilla.
- Add a layer of sliced strawberries on top of the Brie.
- Drizzle balsamic glaze and honey over the strawberries.
- Optionally, add a few fresh basil leaves for extra flavor.

Fold and Cook:
- Fold the tortilla in half, covering the filling.
- Heat a skillet or griddle over medium heat. Brush the surface with a little olive oil.
- Place the quesadilla in the skillet and cook until the tortilla is golden brown and the cheese is melted, usually 2-3 minutes per side.

Repeat:
- Repeat the process with the remaining tortillas and filling.

Slice and Serve:
- Once cooked, remove the quesadillas from the skillet and let them cool for a minute. Slice each quesadilla into wedges.

Enjoy:
- Serve the Strawberry Brie Quesadillas warm and enjoy this delightful combination of sweet strawberries and creamy Brie in a savory quesadilla.

These quesadillas make for a unique and delicious appetizer or light meal. The combination of sweet strawberries, rich Brie cheese, and the tangy balsamic glaze creates a delightful flavor profile.

Strawberry and Feta Salad with Mint

Ingredients:

- 4 cups fresh strawberries, hulled and halved
- 1 cup crumbled feta cheese
- 1/4 cup fresh mint leaves, thinly sliced
- 1/4 cup balsamic glaze
- 2 tablespoons extra-virgin olive oil
- Salt and black pepper, to taste

Instructions:

Prepare Ingredients:
- Hull and halve the fresh strawberries.
- Crumble the feta cheese.
- Thinly slice the fresh mint leaves.

Assemble Salad:
- In a large salad bowl, combine the halved strawberries, crumbled feta cheese, and sliced mint leaves.

Make Dressing:
- In a small bowl, whisk together the balsamic glaze and extra-virgin olive oil until well combined. Season with salt and black pepper to taste.

Dress the Salad:
- Drizzle the balsamic glaze dressing over the strawberry, feta, and mint mixture.

Toss Gently:
- Gently toss the salad to coat the ingredients evenly with the dressing.

Chill (Optional):
- If desired, refrigerate the salad for about 15-30 minutes to allow the flavors to meld.

Serve:
- Serve the Strawberry and Feta Salad with Mint as a refreshing side dish or a light, vibrant appetizer.

This salad offers a perfect balance of sweet strawberries, salty feta cheese, and the refreshing hint of mint, all brought together with a balsamic glaze dressing. It's a delightful and colorful addition to any meal, especially during the warmer seasons. Enjoy!

Strawberry Margarita

Ingredients:

- 2 cups fresh strawberries, hulled
- 1/4 cup fresh lime juice
- 1/4 cup agave syrup or simple syrup (adjust to taste)
- 1 cup tequila
- 1/2 cup triple sec or orange liqueur
- Ice cubes
- Salt or sugar (for rimming glasses, optional)
- Lime wedges (for garnish)

Instructions:

Prepare the Glasses (Optional):
- If desired, rim the glasses with salt or sugar. To do this, moisten the rim of each glass with a lime wedge, then dip it into salt or sugar.

Blend Strawberries:
- In a blender, combine fresh strawberries, lime juice, and agave syrup (or simple syrup). Blend until smooth.

Mix the Margarita:
- In a shaker or pitcher, combine the blended strawberry mixture, tequila, and triple sec. Add ice cubes.

Shake or Stir:
- Shake the mixture well if using a shaker, or stir thoroughly if using a pitcher.

Strain (Optional):
- If you prefer a smoother texture, you can strain the margarita mixture using a fine-mesh sieve to remove strawberry pulp. This step is optional.

Serve:
- Pour the Strawberry Margarita into the prepared glasses over ice.

Garnish:
- Garnish with lime wedges on the rim of the glass or drop one into the drink for extra citrus flavor.

Enjoy Responsibly:
- Sip and enjoy your refreshing Strawberry Margarita responsibly!

This Strawberry Margarita is a delightful twist on the classic cocktail, adding the sweet and vibrant flavors of fresh strawberries. It's perfect for warm weather, parties, or any occasion where you want to enjoy a fruity and refreshing drink. Cheers!

Strawberry and Cucumber Gazpacho

Ingredients:

- 2 cups fresh strawberries, hulled and halved
- 1 large cucumber, peeled and diced
- 1 red bell pepper, seeded and diced
- 1/2 red onion, finely chopped
- 2 cloves garlic, minced
- 3 cups tomato juice or vegetable broth
- 1/4 cup fresh basil leaves, chopped
- 1/4 cup fresh mint leaves, chopped
- 1/4 cup red wine vinegar
- 1/4 cup extra-virgin olive oil
- Salt and pepper to taste
- Optional garnishes: diced cucumber, strawberries, croutons, or a drizzle of balsamic glaze

Instructions:

Prepare Ingredients:
- Hull and halve the strawberries, peel and dice the cucumber, seed and dice the red bell pepper, finely chop the red onion, and mince the garlic.

Blend Ingredients:
- In a blender or food processor, combine the strawberries, cucumber, red bell pepper, red onion, garlic, tomato juice or vegetable broth, basil, mint, red wine vinegar, and olive oil.

Blend Until Smooth:
- Blend the ingredients until you achieve a smooth consistency. You may need to do this in batches, depending on the size of your blender.

Season:
- Season the gazpacho with salt and pepper to taste. Adjust the seasoning according to your preferences.

Chill:
- Refrigerate the gazpacho for at least 2 hours to allow the flavors to meld and to serve it chilled.

Serve:
- Before serving, give the gazpacho a good stir. Ladle it into bowls or glasses.

Garnish (Optional):
- Garnish with diced cucumber, strawberries, croutons, or a drizzle of balsamic glaze for an extra touch.

Enjoy:
- Serve the Strawberry and Cucumber Gazpacho as a refreshing appetizer or light meal. Enjoy the vibrant flavors!

This gazpacho is a perfect choice for hot summer days, providing a cool and satisfying dish with a delightful combination of sweet strawberries, crisp cucumber, and savory vegetables.

Strawberry Ricotta Pancakes

Ingredients:

- 1 cup all-purpose flour
- 1 tablespoon sugar
- 1 teaspoon baking powder
- 1/2 teaspoon baking soda
- 1/4 teaspoon salt
- 1 cup ricotta cheese
- 3/4 cup milk
- 2 large eggs
- 1 teaspoon vanilla extract
- 1 cup fresh strawberries, hulled and chopped
- Butter or oil for cooking
- Maple syrup for serving

Instructions:

Dry Ingredients:
- In a large mixing bowl, whisk together the flour, sugar, baking powder, baking soda, and salt.

Wet Ingredients:
- In a separate bowl, combine the ricotta cheese, milk, eggs, and vanilla extract. Whisk until well combined.

Combine Wet and Dry:
- Pour the wet ingredients into the bowl with the dry ingredients. Stir until just combined. The batter may be slightly lumpy.

Add Strawberries:
- Gently fold in the chopped strawberries into the pancake batter.

Preheat Griddle or Pan:
- Preheat a griddle or non-stick pan over medium heat. Add a small amount of butter or oil to coat the surface.

Cook Pancakes:
- Pour 1/4 cup of batter onto the griddle for each pancake. Cook until bubbles form on the surface, then flip and cook the other side until golden brown.

Repeat:

- Continue cooking the remaining batter in batches. Add more butter or oil as needed.

Serve:
- Serve the Strawberry Ricotta Pancakes warm. Top with additional fresh strawberries and drizzle with maple syrup.

Enjoy:
- Enjoy these delicious and fluffy pancakes as a delightful breakfast treat!

The combination of ricotta cheese and fresh strawberries adds a creamy and fruity twist to traditional pancakes, making them a perfect choice for a special breakfast or brunch.

Strawberry Balsamic Grilled Cheese

Ingredients:

- 8 slices of your favorite bread
- 1/2 cup balsamic reduction (store-bought or homemade)
- 1 cup fresh strawberries, hulled and sliced
- 8 ounces brie cheese, thinly sliced
- Butter for spreading

Instructions:

Prepare Balsamic Reduction:
- If you don't have store-bought balsamic reduction, you can make your own by simmering balsamic vinegar over low heat until it thickens. Let it cool.

Assemble Sandwiches:
- Lay out 4 slices of bread. On each slice, layer brie cheese slices, fresh strawberry slices, and drizzle with balsamic reduction.

Top with Bread:
- Place the remaining 4 slices of bread on top to form sandwiches.

Butter the Bread:
- Spread a thin layer of butter on the outer sides of each sandwich.

Grill:
- Heat a skillet or griddle over medium heat. Once hot, add the sandwiches and cook until the bread is golden brown and the cheese is melted, about 3-4 minutes per side.

Slice and Serve:
- Remove the sandwiches from the skillet and let them rest for a minute. Slice each sandwich in half diagonally.

Enjoy:
- Serve the Strawberry Balsamic Grilled Cheese immediately while warm.

This delightful grilled cheese variation combines the sweetness of fresh strawberries with the rich and creamy brie cheese, enhanced by the tangy balsamic reduction. It's a perfect blend of sweet and savory flavors that will elevate your grilled cheese experience.

Strawberry Basil Chicken

Ingredients:

- 4 boneless, skinless chicken breasts
- Salt and black pepper, to taste
- 1 tablespoon olive oil
- 1 cup fresh strawberries, hulled and sliced
- 2 tablespoons balsamic vinegar
- 1 tablespoon honey
- 1/4 cup fresh basil, chopped
- 1 teaspoon Dijon mustard
- 2 cloves garlic, minced

Instructions:

Season Chicken:
- Season chicken breasts with salt and black pepper on both sides.

Sear Chicken:
- In a large skillet, heat olive oil over medium-high heat. Add chicken breasts and sear until golden brown on both sides and cooked through, about 6-8 minutes per side. Cooking time may vary based on thickness. Ensure the internal temperature reaches 165°F (74°C).

Make Strawberry Basil Sauce:
- In a small bowl, whisk together balsamic vinegar, honey, chopped basil, Dijon mustard, and minced garlic.

Add Strawberries:
- Once the chicken is cooked, reduce heat to low. Pour the strawberry basil sauce over the chicken, and add the sliced strawberries to the skillet.

Simmer:
- Allow the strawberries and sauce to simmer for 2-3 minutes, just until the strawberries are slightly softened and the sauce thickens.

Serve:
- Spoon the strawberry basil sauce over the chicken.

Garnish:
- Garnish with additional fresh basil if desired.

Enjoy:
- Serve the Strawberry Basil Chicken immediately, and enjoy the delightful combination of flavors.

This dish offers a perfect balance of savory and sweet, making it a unique and delicious addition to your meal repertoire.

Strawberry Lemon Muffins

Ingredients:

- 2 cups all-purpose flour
- 1 cup granulated sugar
- 1 tablespoon baking powder
- 1/2 teaspoon baking soda
- 1/4 teaspoon salt
- Zest of 1 lemon
- 1/2 cup unsalted butter, melted and cooled
- 1 cup buttermilk
- 2 large eggs
- 1 teaspoon vanilla extract
- 1 1/2 cups fresh strawberries, diced

For the Glaze:

- 1 cup powdered sugar
- 2-3 tablespoons fresh lemon juice

Instructions:

Preheat Oven:
- Preheat your oven to 375°F (190°C). Line a muffin tin with paper liners or grease each cup.

Mix Dry Ingredients:
- In a large bowl, whisk together the flour, sugar, baking powder, baking soda, and salt.

Add Lemon Zest:
- Stir in the lemon zest to infuse the batter with citrus flavor.

Combine Wet Ingredients:
- In a separate bowl, whisk together the melted butter, buttermilk, eggs, and vanilla extract.

Combine Wet and Dry:
- Pour the wet ingredients into the dry ingredients and gently mix until just combined. Do not overmix; a few lumps are okay.

Fold in Strawberries:

- Gently fold in the diced strawberries, ensuring they are evenly distributed throughout the batter.

Fill Muffin Cups:
- Spoon the batter into the prepared muffin cups, filling each about 2/3 full.

Bake:
- Bake for 18-20 minutes or until a toothpick inserted into the center of a muffin comes out clean.

Cool:
- Allow the muffins to cool in the tin for 5 minutes, then transfer them to a wire rack to cool completely.

Make the Glaze:
- In a small bowl, whisk together the powdered sugar and fresh lemon juice until smooth.

Glaze the Muffins:
- Once the muffins are completely cooled, drizzle the lemon glaze over the top of each muffin.

Enjoy:
- Allow the glaze to set, and then enjoy these delicious Strawberry Lemon Muffins!

These muffins are a perfect blend of sweet strawberries and zesty lemon, making them a delightful treat for breakfast or as a snack.

Strawberry Pistachio Energy Bites

Ingredients:

- 1 cup dried strawberries
- 1 cup rolled oats
- 1/2 cup shelled pistachios
- 1/2 cup honey or maple syrup
- 1/2 cup almond butter or any nut butter of your choice
- 1 teaspoon vanilla extract
- A pinch of salt
- Optional: 1/4 cup chia seeds or flaxseeds for added nutrition

Instructions:

Prepare Ingredients:
- If the dried strawberries are large, you can roughly chop them into smaller pieces. Similarly, chop the pistachios.

Combine Dry Ingredients:
- In a food processor, combine dried strawberries, rolled oats, and shelled pistachios. Pulse until you get a coarse mixture with small pieces.

Add Wet Ingredients:
- Add honey (or maple syrup), almond butter, vanilla extract, and a pinch of salt to the food processor.

Blend:
- Pulse the mixture until it forms a sticky dough. If the mixture seems too dry, you can add a bit more honey or nut butter.

Optional: Add Chia Seeds/Flaxseeds:
- If you'd like to add extra nutritional benefits, pulse in chia seeds or flaxseeds until well combined.

Shape into Bites:
- Scoop out small portions of the mixture and roll them into bite-sized balls using your hands. The mixture might be sticky, so dampen your hands with water if needed.

Chill:
- Place the energy bites on a parchment-lined tray and refrigerate for at least 30 minutes to help them firm up.

Store:

- Once the energy bites have set, transfer them to an airtight container and store in the refrigerator for longer shelf life.

Enjoy:
- Grab these Strawberry Pistachio Energy Bites as a quick snack or a burst of energy before your workout!

These energy bites are not only delicious but also packed with the goodness of strawberries, pistachios, and oats, providing a healthy and convenient snack option.

Strawberry and Spinach Stuffed Chicken Breast

Ingredients:

- 4 boneless, skinless chicken breasts
- Salt and black pepper, to taste
- 1 tablespoon olive oil

For the Strawberry and Spinach Filling:

- 1 cup fresh strawberries, hulled and diced
- 1 cup fresh baby spinach, chopped
- 1/2 cup feta cheese, crumbled
- 1/4 cup balsamic glaze (store-bought or homemade)
- Salt and black pepper, to taste

Instructions:

Preheat the Oven:
- Preheat your oven to 375°F (190°C).

Prepare the Chicken:
- Lay the chicken breasts on a cutting board and make a horizontal slit along the side of each breast to create a pocket. Be careful not to cut all the way through.

Season Chicken:
- Season the inside of each chicken breast with salt and black pepper.

Prepare the Filling:
- In a bowl, combine diced strawberries, chopped spinach, crumbled feta cheese, and balsamic glaze. Mix well. Season with salt and black pepper to taste.

Stuff the Chicken:
- Stuff each chicken breast with the strawberry and spinach mixture, pressing down gently to secure the filling.

Secure with Toothpicks:
- If needed, secure the openings with toothpicks to help hold the stuffing in place.

Sear Chicken:
- In an oven-safe skillet, heat olive oil over medium-high heat. Sear the stuffed chicken breasts for 2-3 minutes on each side until golden brown.

Finish in the Oven:
- Transfer the skillet to the preheated oven and bake for about 20-25 minutes or until the chicken is cooked through, and the internal temperature reaches 165°F (74°C).

Rest and Serve:
- Allow the stuffed chicken breasts to rest for a few minutes before slicing. Remove any toothpicks before serving.

Garnish and Enjoy:
- Garnish with additional fresh strawberries, spinach, or a drizzle of balsamic glaze. Serve these delightful Strawberry and Spinach Stuffed Chicken Breasts with your favorite side dishes.

This recipe combines the sweetness of strawberries with the savory goodness of spinach and feta, creating a delightful flavor profile in each bite. It's a perfect dish for a special dinner or any occasion when you want to impress with a unique and tasty meal!

Strawberry Coconut Chia Popsicles

Ingredients:

- 1 cup fresh strawberries, hulled and halved
- 1/2 cup canned coconut milk
- 2 tablespoons chia seeds
- 1-2 tablespoons honey or maple syrup (adjust to taste)
- 1 teaspoon vanilla extract (optional)

Instructions:

Prepare the Chia Gel:
- In a small bowl, mix chia seeds with 1/4 cup of water. Stir well and let it sit for about 15 minutes, or until the chia seeds absorb the water and form a gel-like consistency.

Blend Strawberries:
- In a blender, combine fresh strawberries, coconut milk, honey or maple syrup, and vanilla extract if using. Blend until smooth.

Combine Strawberry Mixture and Chia Gel:
- In a mixing bowl, combine the strawberry mixture with the prepared chia gel. Stir well to ensure even distribution of chia seeds.

Pour into Popsicle Molds:
- Pour the strawberry-coconut-chia mixture into popsicle molds. Leave a little space at the top for the mixture to expand as it freezes.

Insert Sticks:
- Insert popsicle sticks into the molds.

Freeze:
- Place the popsicle molds in the freezer and let them freeze for at least 4-6 hours, or until completely solid.

Unmold and Enjoy:
- Once the popsicles are fully frozen, remove them from the molds by running warm water over the outside of the molds for a few seconds. Gently pull the popsicles out.

Serve and Enjoy:
- Serve these delightful Strawberry Coconut Chia Popsicles on a hot day as a refreshing and healthy treat.

These popsicles are not only delicious but also packed with the goodness of fresh strawberries and chia seeds. The coconut milk adds a creamy texture, making them a delightful and wholesome frozen treat for summer or any time you crave a cool, fruity snack.

Strawberry and Goat Cheese Grilled Pizza

Ingredients:

- 1 pound pizza dough (store-bought or homemade)
- Olive oil, for brushing
- 1 cup goat cheese, crumbled
- 1 cup fresh strawberries, hulled and sliced
- 1/4 cup balsamic glaze
- Fresh basil leaves, for garnish
- Salt and black pepper, to taste

Instructions:

Preheat the Grill:
- Preheat your grill to medium-high heat.

Prepare the Dough:
- On a lightly floured surface, roll out the pizza dough to your desired thickness.

Brush with Olive Oil:
- Brush one side of the pizza dough with olive oil to prevent sticking on the grill.

Grill the Dough:
- Carefully place the dough, oiled side down, on the preheated grill. Close the lid and grill for 2-3 minutes, or until the bottom is lightly browned and grill marks appear.

Brush the Top with Olive Oil:
- Brush the top of the dough with olive oil and flip it over using tongs or a spatula.

Add Toppings:
- Quickly spread crumbled goat cheese evenly over the grilled side of the dough. Add sliced strawberries on top.

Continue Grilling:
- Close the grill lid and continue cooking for an additional 3-4 minutes, or until the cheese is melted, and the crust is golden brown.

Drizzle with Balsamic Glaze:
- Remove the pizza from the grill and drizzle with balsamic glaze.

Season and Garnish:

- Season with salt and black pepper to taste. Garnish with fresh basil leaves.

Slice and Serve:
- Slice the grilled pizza into portions and serve immediately while it's hot.

This Strawberry and Goat Cheese Grilled Pizza offers a delightful combination of sweet and savory flavors. The creamy goat cheese pairs perfectly with the sweetness of fresh strawberries, and the balsamic glaze adds a tangy kick. It's a perfect dish for a summer evening or anytime you want to enjoy a unique and delicious pizza experience.

Strawberry Balsamic Glazed Salmon

Ingredients:

- 4 salmon fillets
- Salt and black pepper, to taste
- 1 tablespoon olive oil

For the Strawberry Balsamic Glaze:

- 1 cup fresh strawberries, hulled and chopped
- 2 tablespoons balsamic vinegar
- 1 tablespoon honey
- 1 teaspoon Dijon mustard
- Salt and black pepper, to taste

Instructions:

Season and Sear the Salmon:
- Season the salmon fillets with salt and black pepper. In a skillet over medium-high heat, add olive oil. Sear the salmon fillets for 3-4 minutes on each side or until they are cooked to your preferred doneness. Remove from the skillet and set aside.

Prepare the Glaze:
- In the same skillet, add chopped strawberries, balsamic vinegar, honey, Dijon mustard, salt, and black pepper. Stir well and bring the mixture to a simmer.

Simmer and Thicken:
- Allow the glaze to simmer for 5-7 minutes, or until the strawberries break down, and the sauce thickens.

Glaze the Salmon:
- Return the seared salmon fillets to the skillet, spooning the strawberry balsamic glaze over the top. Cook for an additional 2-3 minutes, allowing the salmon to absorb the flavors of the glaze.

Serve:
- Once the salmon is fully glazed and cooked, transfer the fillets to plates. Drizzle any remaining glaze over the top.

Garnish (Optional):
- Garnish with additional fresh strawberries or herbs if desired.

Enjoy:
- Serve the Strawberry Balsamic Glazed Salmon immediately while it's warm. It pairs well with a side of steamed vegetables, rice, or quinoa.

This recipe offers a delightful combination of the savory richness of salmon with the sweet and tangy flavor of strawberry balsamic glaze. It's a unique and refreshing way to enjoy salmon, perfect for a special meal or a dinner with a touch of elegance.

Strawberry and Cream Cheese Stuffed French Toast Casserole

Ingredients:

For the Casserole:

- 1 loaf of French bread, cut into cubes
- 1 cup fresh strawberries, hulled and sliced
- 1 cup cream cheese, softened
- 8 large eggs
- 2 cups whole milk
- 1/2 cup heavy cream
- 1/2 cup granulated sugar
- 1/4 cup maple syrup
- 1 teaspoon vanilla extract
- 1/2 teaspoon ground cinnamon
- Pinch of salt

For the Topping:

- 1/2 cup all-purpose flour
- 1/2 cup brown sugar, packed
- 1/4 cup cold unsalted butter, cut into small pieces
- Powdered sugar for dusting (optional)
- Maple syrup for serving

Instructions:

    Prepare the Casserole:
- Grease a 9x13-inch baking dish. Arrange half of the French bread cubes in the bottom of the dish.

    Add Strawberries and Cream Cheese:
- Sprinkle half of the sliced strawberries over the bread cubes. Drop spoonfuls of softened cream cheese evenly over the strawberries.

    Layer with More Bread and Strawberries:
- Add the remaining French bread cubes on top, followed by the remaining strawberries.

    Prepare the Custard Mixture:

- In a large mixing bowl, whisk together the eggs, whole milk, heavy cream, granulated sugar, maple syrup, vanilla extract, ground cinnamon, and a pinch of salt.

Pour Over the Bread:
- Pour the custard mixture evenly over the bread and strawberry layers, ensuring all the bread is soaked. Press down gently to help the bread absorb the liquid.

Cover and Refrigerate:
- Cover the baking dish with plastic wrap and refrigerate for at least 4 hours or overnight. This allows the flavors to meld and the bread to soak up the custard.

Preheat the Oven:
- Preheat your oven to 350°F (175°C).

Prepare the Topping:
- In a small bowl, combine the flour, brown sugar, and cold butter pieces. Use a fork or your fingers to create a crumbly texture.

Bake the Casserole:
- Sprinkle the crumb topping evenly over the soaked bread mixture. Bake in the preheated oven for 45-50 minutes or until the top is golden brown, and the center is set.

Serve:
- Remove from the oven and let it cool for a few minutes. Dust with powdered sugar if desired. Serve slices of the Strawberry and Cream Cheese Stuffed French Toast Casserole with maple syrup.

This casserole is perfect for breakfast or brunch, especially for a special occasion or when you have guests. Enjoy the delightful combination of creamy cream cheese, sweet strawberries, and perfectly soaked French bread in every bite!

Strawberry Rhubarb Crisp

Ingredients:

For the Filling:

- 3 cups fresh rhubarb, chopped
- 3 cups fresh strawberries, hulled and halved
- 1 cup granulated sugar
- 2 tablespoons cornstarch
- 1 teaspoon vanilla extract
- Zest of 1 orange (optional)

For the Topping:

- 1 cup old-fashioned rolled oats
- 1/2 cup all-purpose flour
- 1/2 cup packed brown sugar
- 1/2 teaspoon ground cinnamon
- 1/4 teaspoon salt
- 1/2 cup unsalted butter, cold and cut into small pieces

Instructions:

Preheat the Oven:
- Preheat your oven to 350°F (175°C). Grease a 9x13-inch baking dish.

Prepare the Filling:
- In a large bowl, combine the chopped rhubarb, halved strawberries, granulated sugar, cornstarch, vanilla extract, and orange zest. Toss everything together until the fruit is evenly coated.

Transfer to Baking Dish:
- Spread the fruit mixture evenly in the prepared baking dish.

Prepare the Topping:
- In a separate bowl, combine the rolled oats, flour, brown sugar, ground cinnamon, and salt. Add the cold butter pieces and use your fingers or a pastry cutter to incorporate the butter into the dry ingredients until you have a crumbly texture.

Top the Fruit:
- Sprinkle the oat topping evenly over the strawberry and rhubarb filling.

Bake:
- Bake in the preheated oven for 40-45 minutes or until the fruit is bubbling, and the topping is golden brown.

Cool and Serve:
- Allow the crisp to cool for a few minutes before serving. It can be served warm on its own or with a scoop of vanilla ice cream or a dollop of whipped cream.

Enjoy:
- Enjoy the Strawberry Rhubarb Crisp as a delightful dessert, showcasing the perfect balance of sweet strawberries and tart rhubarb with a crunchy oat topping.

This Strawberry Rhubarb Crisp is a classic and comforting dessert, especially popular during the spring and early summer when strawberries and rhubarb are in season. The combination of the sweet and juicy berries with the tangy rhubarb creates a mouthwatering treat that's perfect for sharing with family and friends.

Strawberry and Avocado Chicken Salad

Ingredients:

For the Salad:

- 2 cups cooked chicken breast, shredded or diced
- 2 cups fresh strawberries, hulled and sliced
- 1 ripe avocado, peeled, pitted, and diced
- 1/2 cup red onion, finely sliced
- 1/4 cup fresh basil leaves, thinly sliced
- 4 cups mixed salad greens (lettuce, spinach, arugula, or your choice)

For the Dressing:

- 3 tablespoons balsamic vinegar
- 2 tablespoons extra-virgin olive oil
- 1 tablespoon honey
- 1 teaspoon Dijon mustard
- Salt and pepper to taste

Optional Toppings:

- 1/4 cup crumbled feta or goat cheese
- 1/4 cup chopped pecans or walnuts

Instructions:

Prepare the Salad:
- In a large salad bowl, combine the shredded or diced chicken, sliced strawberries, diced avocado, sliced red onion, and fresh basil leaves.

Prepare the Dressing:
- In a small bowl, whisk together the balsamic vinegar, extra-virgin olive oil, honey, Dijon mustard, salt, and pepper until well combined.

Assemble the Salad:
- Pour the dressing over the salad ingredients in the large bowl. Gently toss everything together until the salad is well coated with the dressing.

Serve:
- Arrange the mixed salad greens on serving plates or a platter. Spoon the strawberry and avocado chicken mixture over the greens.

Optional Toppings:
- If desired, sprinkle crumbled feta or goat cheese and chopped pecans or walnuts over the top for added flavor and texture.

Enjoy:
- Serve the Strawberry and Avocado Chicken Salad immediately as a light and satisfying meal. The combination of sweet strawberries, creamy avocado, and savory chicken creates a delightful balance of flavors.

This Strawberry and Avocado Chicken Salad is not only delicious but also packed with nutrients. It's perfect for a quick and healthy lunch or dinner, especially during the warmer months when strawberries are in season. Feel free to customize the salad with your favorite greens and toppings.

Strawberry and Pecan Quinoa Salad

Ingredients:

For the Salad:

- 1 cup quinoa, rinsed and cooked according to package instructions
- 2 cups fresh strawberries, hulled and sliced
- 1/2 cup pecans, toasted and chopped
- 1/4 cup red onion, finely chopped
- 1/4 cup fresh mint leaves, chopped
- 1/4 cup crumbled feta cheese (optional)
- Mixed salad greens (lettuce, spinach, arugula, or your choice)

For the Dressing:

- 3 tablespoons balsamic vinegar
- 2 tablespoons extra-virgin olive oil
- 1 tablespoon honey
- 1 teaspoon Dijon mustard
- Salt and pepper to taste

Instructions:

Prepare the Quinoa:
- Rinse the quinoa under cold water. Cook it according to the package instructions. Once cooked, fluff it with a fork and let it cool to room temperature.

Toast the Pecans:
- In a dry skillet over medium heat, toast the pecans for a few minutes until they become fragrant. Be careful not to burn them. Remove from heat and let them cool before chopping.

Prepare the Dressing:
- In a small bowl, whisk together balsamic vinegar, extra-virgin olive oil, honey, Dijon mustard, salt, and pepper until well combined.

Assemble the Salad:
- In a large salad bowl, combine the cooked quinoa, sliced strawberries, chopped toasted pecans, red onion, and fresh mint. If desired, add crumbled feta cheese for an extra burst of flavor.

Add the Dressing:
- Pour the balsamic dressing over the salad ingredients. Gently toss everything together until the salad is well coated with the dressing.

Serve:
- Arrange the mixed salad greens on serving plates or a platter. Spoon the quinoa and strawberry mixture over the greens.

Enjoy:
- Serve the Strawberry and Pecan Quinoa Salad immediately, offering a delightful blend of sweet strawberries, nutty pecans, and the wholesome goodness of quinoa. It's a perfect choice for a light and nutritious meal.

Feel free to customize this salad by adding your favorite herbs, greens, or additional toppings. It's a versatile dish that can be enjoyed as a refreshing lunch or a side dish for dinner.

Strawberry and Nutella Crepes

Ingredients:

For the Crepes:

- 1 cup all-purpose flour
- 2 large eggs
- 1 cup milk
- 1/2 cup water
- 2 tablespoons melted butter
- 1 tablespoon sugar
- 1/2 teaspoon vanilla extract
- Pinch of salt

For Filling and Topping:

- Nutella (as needed)
- Fresh strawberries, hulled and sliced
- Powdered sugar (for dusting)
- Whipped cream (optional)

Instructions:

1. Prepare the Crepe Batter:

- In a blender, combine the flour, eggs, milk, water, melted butter, sugar, vanilla extract, and a pinch of salt. Blend until smooth. Let the batter rest in the refrigerator for at least 30 minutes.

2. Cook the Crepes:

- Heat a non-stick skillet or crepe pan over medium heat. Lightly grease the pan with butter or cooking spray.
- Pour a small amount of batter into the center of the pan, swirling it to spread evenly. Cook for about 1-2 minutes until the edges begin to lift, then flip and cook the other side for an additional 1-2 minutes. Repeat until all the batter is used.

3. Assemble the Crepes:

- Spread a thin layer of Nutella on each crepe, leaving a border around the edges.
- Place sliced strawberries on one half of the crepe.

4. Fold and Serve:

- Fold the crepe in half over the strawberries, then fold it in half again to create a triangle.
- Repeat with the remaining crepes.

5. Garnish and Enjoy:

- Place the folded crepes on serving plates. Garnish with additional sliced strawberries, a dusting of powdered sugar, and a dollop of whipped cream if desired.

6. Serve Warm:

- Serve the Strawberry and Nutella Crepes warm, allowing the Nutella to melt slightly and the strawberries to release their juices.

This delightful dessert or breakfast treat combines the rich, chocolaty flavor of Nutella with the sweetness of fresh strawberries, all wrapped in delicate, thin crepes. It's a crowd-pleaser and perfect for any occasion. Feel free to get creative with additional toppings such as chopped nuts or a drizzle of chocolate sauce. Enjoy!

Strawberry Basil Lemon Sorbet

Ingredients:

- 2 cups fresh strawberries, hulled and halved
- 1/2 cup fresh basil leaves, packed
- 1 cup granulated sugar
- 1 cup water
- 1/2 cup freshly squeezed lemon juice (about 3-4 lemons)
- Zest of 1 lemon

Instructions:

Prepare Simple Syrup:
- In a saucepan, combine the granulated sugar and water. Heat over medium heat, stirring occasionally, until the sugar completely dissolves. Bring the mixture to a gentle boil, then remove it from heat. Allow the simple syrup to cool.

Infuse with Basil:
- Add the fresh basil leaves to the simple syrup. Let it steep for at least 20-30 minutes to infuse the basil flavor into the syrup. You can adjust the steeping time based on how strong you want the basil flavor.

Blend the Strawberries:
- In a blender or food processor, blend the fresh strawberries until smooth.

Strain the Basil Syrup:
- Strain the basil leaves from the simple syrup to leave a clear liquid.

Combine Ingredients:
- In a bowl, combine the strawberry puree, basil-infused simple syrup, freshly squeezed lemon juice, and lemon zest. Mix well.

Chill the Mixture:
- Refrigerate the mixture for at least 2-3 hours or until it's well-chilled.

Freeze in an Ice Cream Maker:
- Transfer the chilled mixture to an ice cream maker and churn according to the manufacturer's instructions until it reaches a sorbet consistency.

Transfer to a Container:
- Transfer the sorbet to a lidded container and freeze for an additional 2-3 hours to firm up.

Serve and Enjoy:

- Scoop the Strawberry Basil Lemon Sorbet into bowls or cones. Garnish with fresh basil leaves or a slice of lemon if desired.

This sorbet combines the sweetness of strawberries with the bright, citrusy notes of lemon and a hint of basil for a unique and delightful frozen treat. It's perfect for cooling down on a hot day or serving as a refreshing palate cleanser between courses. Enjoy!

Strawberry Cinnamon Rolls

Ingredients:

For the Dough:

- 1 cup warm milk (about 110°F or 43°C)
- 2 1/4 teaspoons active dry yeast (1 packet)
- 1/2 cup granulated sugar
- 1/3 cup unsalted butter, melted
- 4 cups all-purpose flour
- 1/2 teaspoon salt
- 2 large eggs

For the Filling:

- 1/3 cup unsalted butter, softened
- 1 cup granulated sugar
- 2 cups fresh strawberries, hulled and sliced
- 1 tablespoon ground cinnamon

For the Cream Cheese Frosting:

- 1/2 cup unsalted butter, softened
- 4 ounces cream cheese, softened
- 2 cups powdered sugar
- 1 teaspoon vanilla extract

Instructions:

Activate the Yeast:
- In a bowl, combine the warm milk, active dry yeast, and a pinch of sugar. Let it sit for about 5-10 minutes until the mixture becomes frothy.

Prepare the Dough:
- In a large mixing bowl, combine the activated yeast mixture, melted butter, sugar, salt, and eggs. Gradually add the flour and mix until a dough forms.

Knead the Dough:

- Turn the dough out onto a floured surface and knead for about 5-8 minutes until it becomes smooth and elastic.

First Rise:
- Place the dough in a greased bowl, cover it with a clean kitchen towel, and let it rise in a warm place for 1-2 hours or until it doubles in size.

Roll Out the Dough:
- Punch down the risen dough and roll it out on a floured surface into a rectangle (about 16x20 inches).

Spread Filling:
- Spread the softened butter over the rolled-out dough. Mix together the sugar and ground cinnamon, then sprinkle it evenly over the butter. Arrange the sliced strawberries on top.

Roll and Cut:
- Starting from the long edge, tightly roll the dough into a log. Slice the log into 12 equal pieces.

Second Rise:
- Place the cut rolls in a greased baking dish, cover with a towel, and let them rise for another 30-45 minutes.

Bake:
- Preheat the oven to 350°F (175°C). Bake the rolls for 25-30 minutes or until they are golden brown.

Make the Frosting:
- While the rolls are baking, prepare the cream cheese frosting by beating together the softened butter, cream cheese, powdered sugar, and vanilla extract until smooth.

Frost the Rolls:
- Once the rolls are out of the oven and slightly cooled, spread the cream cheese frosting over the top.

Serve and Enjoy:
- Serve the Strawberry Cinnamon Rolls warm and enjoy the delicious combination of sweet strawberries and cinnamon.

These Strawberry Cinnamon Rolls are a delightful twist on the classic cinnamon roll, adding the freshness of strawberries to the sweet and spiced filling. Perfect for breakfast or a sweet treat any time of the day!

Strawberry and Almond Butter Smoothie

Ingredients:

- 1 cup fresh or frozen strawberries (hulled)
- 1 banana, peeled
- 2 tablespoons almond butter
- 1 cup almond milk (or any milk of your choice)
- 1 tablespoon honey or maple syrup (optional, depending on sweetness preference)
- Ice cubes (optional)

Instructions:

Prepare the Ingredients:
- If using fresh strawberries, hull them. Peel the banana.

Combine Ingredients:
- In a blender, combine the fresh or frozen strawberries, peeled banana, almond butter, almond milk, and honey (if using).

Blend Until Smooth:
- Blend the ingredients until smooth and creamy. If you prefer a thicker smoothie, you can add ice cubes and blend again.

Taste and Adjust:
- Taste the smoothie and adjust the sweetness if needed by adding more honey or maple syrup.

Serve:
- Pour the smoothie into glasses and serve immediately.

Optional Garnish:
- Garnish with sliced strawberries or a drizzle of almond butter if desired.

This Strawberry and Almond Butter Smoothie is not only delicious but also packed with nutrients. The combination of sweet strawberries, creamy almond butter, and banana creates a satisfying and wholesome drink. Enjoy it for breakfast, as a snack, or whenever you're in the mood for a refreshing and nutritious beverage!

Strawberry Pistachio Salad

Ingredients:

- 6 cups mixed salad greens (spinach, arugula, or your choice)
- 1 cup fresh strawberries, hulled and sliced
- 1/2 cup crumbled feta cheese
- 1/3 cup shelled pistachios, chopped
- 1/4 cup red onion, thinly sliced
- Balsamic vinaigrette dressing (store-bought or homemade)
- Salt and pepper to taste

Instructions:

Prepare the Salad Greens:
- Wash and dry the salad greens thoroughly. If using large leaves, you can tear them into bite-sized pieces.

Slice the Strawberries:
- Hull the strawberries and slice them into thin rounds.

Assemble the Salad:
- In a large salad bowl, combine the mixed greens, sliced strawberries, crumbled feta cheese, chopped pistachios, and thinly sliced red onion.

Toss the Salad:
- Gently toss the salad ingredients to combine them evenly.

Dress the Salad:
- Drizzle balsamic vinaigrette dressing over the salad. Start with a small amount and add more according to your taste preference.

Season with Salt and Pepper:
- Season the salad with a pinch of salt and pepper. Adjust the seasoning as needed.

Serve:
- Divide the salad among plates or serve it in the bowl.

Optional Garnish:
- If desired, garnish with additional chopped pistachios on top.

This Strawberry Pistachio Salad is a delightful combination of sweet strawberries, salty feta, crunchy pistachios, and the freshness of mixed greens. It's a perfect side dish for a light lunch or dinner. Enjoy!

Strawberry and Balsamic Bruschetta

Ingredients:

- 1 French baguette, sliced into 1/2-inch thick rounds
- 1 cup fresh strawberries, hulled and diced
- 1/4 cup fresh basil leaves, thinly sliced
- 1/3 cup balsamic glaze
- 1/2 cup goat cheese, crumbled
- 2 tablespoons extra-virgin olive oil
- Salt and black pepper to taste

Instructions:

Preheat the Oven:
- Preheat your oven to 375°F (190°C).

Toast the Baguette:
- Place the baguette slices on a baking sheet. Toast them in the preheated oven for about 5-7 minutes or until they are golden and crisp. Remove from the oven and let them cool slightly.

Prepare the Strawberry Mixture:
- In a bowl, combine the diced strawberries and thinly sliced basil. Drizzle half of the balsamic glaze over the mixture and gently toss to coat. Set aside.

Assemble the Bruschetta:
- Spread a generous layer of crumbled goat cheese on each toasted baguette slice.

Top with Strawberry Mixture:
- Spoon the strawberry and basil mixture over the goat cheese-covered baguette slices.

Drizzle with Balsamic Glaze:
- Drizzle the remaining balsamic glaze over the top of each bruschetta.

Season and Serve:
- Drizzle extra-virgin olive oil over the bruschetta and season with salt and black pepper to taste.

Serve Immediately:
- Arrange the Strawberry and Balsamic Bruschetta on a serving platter and serve immediately.

This Strawberry and Balsamic Bruschetta is a delightful appetizer that combines the sweetness of strawberries with the tangy balsamic glaze and creamy goat cheese. It's perfect for a light and refreshing snack or as an appetizer for gatherings. Enjoy!

Strawberry Tiramisu

Ingredients:

- 1 pound fresh strawberries, hulled and sliced
- 1/2 cup granulated sugar
- 1 tablespoon lemon juice
- 1 cup strong brewed coffee, cooled to room temperature
- 3 tablespoons coffee liqueur (e.g., Kahlúa)
- 3 large egg yolks
- 1 cup granulated sugar
- 1 1/2 cups mascarpone cheese, softened
- 1 teaspoon vanilla extract
- 1 1/2 cups heavy cream
- 24-30 ladyfinger cookies (savoiardi)
- Cocoa powder, for dusting
- Fresh mint leaves, for garnish (optional)

Instructions:

Prepare the Strawberry Sauce:
- In a medium bowl, combine the sliced strawberries, 1/2 cup sugar, and lemon juice. Toss gently to coat the strawberries, then set aside to macerate for at least 30 minutes. This will create a flavorful strawberry sauce.

Prepare the Coffee Mixture:
- In a shallow dish, mix the brewed coffee and coffee liqueur. Set aside.

Prepare the Mascarpone Filling:
- In a large bowl, whisk together the egg yolks and 1 cup sugar until well combined and slightly thickened.
- Add the softened mascarpone cheese and vanilla extract. Mix until smooth and well incorporated.

Whip the Cream:
- In a separate bowl, whip the heavy cream until stiff peaks form.

Combine the Ingredients:
- Gently fold the whipped cream into the mascarpone mixture until smooth and airy.

Assemble the Tiramisu:

- Dip each ladyfinger into the coffee mixture, ensuring they are coated but not soaked.
- Arrange a layer of dipped ladyfingers in the bottom of a serving dish or individual glasses.

Add the Mascarpone Mixture and Strawberries:
- Spread a portion of the mascarpone mixture over the ladyfingers.
- Spoon a layer of macerated strawberries over the mascarpone.

Repeat the Layers:
- Repeat the process, creating layers with dipped ladyfingers, mascarpone mixture, and strawberries until you reach the top of the dish.

Chill:
- Cover the tiramisu and refrigerate for at least 4 hours or preferably overnight to allow the flavors to meld.

Serve:
- Before serving, dust the top with cocoa powder and garnish with fresh mint leaves if desired.

Enjoy:
- Serve chilled and enjoy this delightful Strawberry Tiramisu!

This Strawberry Tiramisu is a fruity twist on the classic Italian dessert, and it's sure to impress with its layers of coffee-soaked ladyfingers, mascarpone cream, and sweet strawberries. Perfect for a refreshing and elegant dessert!

www.ingramcontent.com/pod-product-compliance
Lightning Source LLC
LaVergne TN
LVHW062048070526
838201LV00080B/2187